125 Brain Games for Toddlers and Twos:

Simple Games to Promote Early Brain Development, Revised

by Jackie Silberg
with contributions from Keith Pentz

Also by Jackie Silberg:

125 Brain Games for Babies: Simple Games to Promote Early Brain Development, Revised

300 Three Minute Games: Quick and Easy Activities for 2–5 Year Olds

500 Five Minute Games: Quick and Easy Activities for 3–6 Year Olds

All About Me

Baby Smarts: Games for Playing and Learning

Brain Games for Babies, Toddlers, and Twos: 140 Fun Ways to Boost Development

The Complete Book of Activities, Games, Stories, Props, Recipes, and Dances for Young Children: Over 600 Selections, with Pam Schiller

The Complete Book of Rhymes, Songs, Poems, Fingerplays, and Chants: Over 700 Selections, with Pam Schiller

Games to Play with Babies, Third Edition

Games to Play with Toddlers, Revised

Games to Play with Two-Year-Olds, Revised

Go Anywhere Games for Babies

Hello Rhythm: Rhythm Activities, Songs, and Games to Develop Skills

Hello Sound: Creative Music Activities for Parents and Teachers of Young Children

Higglety, Pigglety, Pop! 233 Playful Rhymes and Chants

The I Can't Sing Book: For Grownups Who Can't Carry a Tune in a Paper Bag… But Want to Do Music with Young Children

I Live in Kansas

I Love Children Songbook

Learning Games: Exploring the Senses Through Play

The Learning Power of Laughter

Let's Be Friends

Lollipops and Spaghetti Activity Book: Developmental Activities

My Toes Are Starting to Wiggle! And Other Easy Songs for Circle Time

Peanut Butter, Tarzan, and Roosters Activity Book

Reading Games

Sing Yeladim

Sniggles, Squirrels, and Chickenpox: 40 Original Songs with Activities for Early Childhood

Songs to Sing with Babies

BRAIN GAMES

Revised

for Toddlers
and Twos

Jackie Silberg

with Contributions from **Keith Pentz**

Published by Gryphon House, Inc.
PO Box 10, Lewisville, NC 27023
800.638.0928; 877.638.7576 (fax)

Visit us on the web at www.gryphonhouse.com.

Reprinted January 2019

Library of Congress Cataloging-in-Publication Data
Silberg, Jackie, 1934-
   125 brain games for toddlers and twos / Jackie Silberg. --2nd. ed.
     p. cm.
   Summary: "Revised and updated with more than 50 new games and the latest brain research, this book is filled with activities to promote brain development for children from 12 to 36 months"--Provided by publisher.
ISBN 978-0-87659-392-9 (pbk.)
1. Games. 2. Educational games. 3. Toddlers. I. Title. II. Title: One hundred twenty-five brain games for toddlers and twos.
GV1203.s532 2012
649'.5--dc23   2011049682

Bulk Purchase
Gryphon House books are available for special premiums and sales promotions as well as for fund-raising use. Special editions or book excerpts also can be created to specifications. For details, contact the Director of Marketing at Gryphon House.

Disclaimer
Gryphon House, Inc. cannot be held responsible for damage, mishap, or injury incurred during the use of or because of activities in this book. Appropriate and reasonable caution and adult supervision of children involved in activities and corresponding to the age and capability of each child involved is recommended at all times. Do not leave children unattended at any time. Observe safety and caution at all times.

Table of Contents

Introduction

Playing with toddlers and two-year-olds is delightful. These little ones are affectionate, assertive, bouncy, challenging, curious, enchanting, energetic, funny, independent, and joyful.

During the first three years of life, the brain is forming connections that will determine a lifetime of skills and potential. Everyone who cares for toddlers and twos has a role in ensuring that these early years include interesting activities and experiences that safely stimulate young children's optimal development.

The quality of early experiences influences children's brain structure for life. The brain continues to grow and develop after birth. Brain development consists of an ongoing process of wiring and rewiring the connections among neurons. Although this happens throughout life, in early childhood the brain is genetically programmed to produce more synapses than it will ultimately use. Pruning allows the brain to keep the connections that have a purpose, while eliminating those that don't. Pruning increases the efficiency with which the brain can do what it needs to do.

By the time a child is three years old, her brain has formed about one thousand trillion connections—about twice as many as adults have. A baby's brain is superdense and will stay that way throughout the first decade of life. Some brain cells, called neurons, are hardwired to other brain cells before birth. These neurons control your child's heartbeat, breathing, and reflexes and regulate other functions essential to survival. The rest of the brain connections are just waiting to be "hooked up." Brain cells are entirely planned for making connections. Each cell sends signals out to other brain cells and receives input from other cells. These signals, in the form of electrical impulses, travel down the length of the nerve cell. Certain chemicals (such as serotonin) travel from cell to cell, creating connections. A single cell can connect with as many as fifteen thousand other cells. The incredibly complex network of connections that results is often referred to as the brain's "wiring" or "circuitry." The connections neurons make with one another are called synapses. The receptive branches of the nerve cells, called dendrites, are growing and reaching out to form trillions upon trillions of synapses. The brain's weight triples to nearly adult size. While various parts of the brain develop at different rates, study after study has shown that the peak production period for synapses is from birth to about age 10.

The very best way to develop young children's brain connections is to give children what they need, which is an environment that is safe, is interesting to explore, and is filled with people who will respond to their emotional and intellectual needs. Brain research supports what we already know: Young children need loving, supportive people in their lives who will sing to them, hug them, talk to them, and read to them. All the games in this book develop the brain capacity of toddlers and two-year-olds. They are the building blocks for future learning—a good, solid beginning for little ones, filled with experiences that are also fun and enjoyable. Each game in the book refers to related brain research. We can help children grow and learn by asking them meaningful questions; by exposing them to a variety of experiences, activities, and toys; and of course, by giving them love and security.

This book is about helping to "grow" the brains of young children by playing meaningful games with them. Whether it is through singing, dancing, cuddling, rocking, talking, smelling, or tasting, you can encourage the pathways of children's brains to make new connections.

With all of the new brain research, we can learn invaluable insights into the evolution of the senses, motor skills, social and emotional growth, memory skills, language development, and intelligence.

But most importantly, we can finally understand how great the contributions of family members, early childhood teachers, and caregivers can be to the development of young children's brains.

Push Me, Pull You

- Sit with your little one on the floor, face-to-face.
- Sit close together so you can hold hands with your child.
- Hold both of your child's hands, and gently rock back and forth.
- As you lean backward, gently and slowly pull your little one toward you.
- Repeat the rocking action. This time, as you hold hands with your little one, let him lean back and "pull" you.

What brain research says

Attachment and bonding are critical in the early months and years of life. The social and emotional skills a child develops will determine the quality of his engagement with the world throughout life.

Lots of TLC

- This game develops your toddler's nurturing skills.
- Sit on the floor with your toddler, and put two or three of your toddler's favorite stuffed animals on the floor with you.
- Pick up one of the stuffed toys and cuddle it in your arms. Say loving words such as, "Playing with you is so much fun," "I love your brown fur," or "I love to hug you."
- Now let your child do the same thing.
  - Give your child one of the animals, and ask her to cuddle it and give it kisses.
  - Keep the game going as long as your toddler is interested. Your toddler will soon be playing this game by herself.

What brain research says

According to Dr. Bruce Perry, a psychiatrist at Baylor College of Medicine, children who do not get enough loving cuddles early in life may lack the brain wiring to form close relationships.

Crawl to the Toy

- When your toddler has started crawling, encourage him with the following game.
- Place a favorite toy at one end of the room.
- Get down on the floor, and crawl to the toy. When you reach the toy, pick it up, and pretend that it says, "Come on (child's name), can you come get me?"
- Encourage your little one to crawl to the toy.
- If your child is getting ready to walk, place the toy higher up so he must pull himself up to reach the toy.
- It is also a lot of fun to crawl around in a circle with your child.

What brain research says

Crawling is a key developmental milestone that also develops and strengthens neural connections in the brain.

Rock-a-Bye, Baby

● Hold your child in your arms, and rock her back and forth as you sing lullabies and other soothing songs, such as the following:

"Goodnight, Irene"
"Hush, Little Baby" ("The Mockingbird Song")
"Kum Ba Ya"
"Rock-a-bye, Baby"
"Swing Low, Sweet Chariot"

● If you do not know the words to a song, just hum a soft melody.
● Rock back and forth as you sing. This will usually calm your child and will develop your child's trust in you.
● At the end of the song, hold your toddler close, and give her a big hug.

What brain research says

Studies have shown that exposure to music improves spatial-temporal reasoning, which is the ability to see a disassembled picture and mentally piece it back together. Math skills depend on this kind of reasoning.

Reading Games

● There are many ways you can help your toddler develop a love of books and reading, including the following:

- Encourage your toddler to look at books such as *Pat the Bunny*, Dorothy Kunhardt's classic touch-and-feel book, and sturdy cardboard or cloth books.
- Point to pictures in books, and name what you see in the pictures.
- Sing the nursery rhymes in books.
- Vary the tone of your voice, make funny faces, or do other special effects when you read books, to stimulate your child's interest in books and stories.
- Read to your toddler often, but for short periods of time.

What brain research says

Reading or telling a story to your child will help "grow" his brain and encourage him to associate books with what he loves the most—your voice and closeness.

All About Me

- Play a simple game of learning about the body with your little one.
- As you say a particular part of the body, ask your little one to point to that part.
- Once your little one knows some of the words for the parts of the body, invite her to say the body part as you touch it.

What brain research says

When you say the name of each part of the body over and over, connections will form in the brain that will allow a child to learn the names of each part of the body. From birth, the brain creates these connections that form our habits, our language, and our thoughts.

Song Patting

- Try Song Patting when changing your toddler's diaper, giving him a bath, or anytime.
- Sing your favorite song (It can be any song!) to your toddler, and at the same time, pat his tummy or back with your index finger to the rhythm of the song.
- Always end the song with a snuggly kiss.
- You can also sing one line of the song and pat one word in that line. For example, "Twinkle, twinkle, little (pat your child for the word *star*, but do not sing it)."
- This game helps develop your child's sense of rhythm and his listening skills.

What brain research says

For a young child's brain to grow and thrive, he needs to be loved, held, talked to, read to, and allowed to explore his environment.

Feel the Beat

- Play some music or sing your child's favorite song (or your favorite song) to your little one.
- Help her feel the rhythm and beat by holding and dancing with your child, clapping the rhythm, or taking your child's hands and clapping them together in time to the music.
- For more fun, add a shaker or another sound-maker (for instance, tap two wooden or metal spoons together) to support the rhythm.

What brain research says

Music helps to instill a sense of pattern, which is important for learning math skills. Recognizing patterns strengthens pathways in the brain.

Go to Bed Late

- Hold your toddler in your lap, and say the following rhyme. Hold his hands up high in the air when you say the word *tall* and down to his toes when you say the word *small*.

  Go to bed late,
  You will stay very small.
  Go to bed early,
  You will grow very tall.

- You can also hold your toddler while you are standing. This time hold him high in the air when you say the word *tall* and down to the ground when you say the word *small*.

- Doing things with your toddler that you both enjoy is a great way to form a strong bond between you.

What brain research says

Children who have loving, consistent, sensitive caretakers will develop stronger social and cognitive skills than children who do not benefit from such care.

Part of the Community

- Teach and encourage your little one to wave hello and goodbye.
- Even if your child does not yet communicate with many words, teach your little one a few signs.

eat

again

more

drink

- Teaching your child multiple methods for communication will help her develop her self-confidence and will give her a sense of belonging.

What brain research says

Trusting relationships create a supportive environment where brain development can thrive.

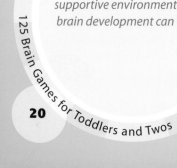

The Singsong Game

- This delightful game enhances a child's language skills.
- Instead of speaking words in your regular voice, try using a singsong voice. Sing the sounds of the words upward and then downward.
- For example, sing sentences such as, "Let's go play with blocks," or "I am going to catch you."
- Another way to use a singsong voice is to sing, "Naa naa naa naa naa naa," to the same melody as "Ring Around the Rosie."
- Sit on the floor with your toddler, and put one of his favorite stuffed toys in your lap. Sing to the toy in your singsong voice, and then give the toy to your little one.
- He will try to copy you, and you will soon hear your toddler playing the same game when he is by himself.

What brain research says

Talking to a young child increases the number of words that he will recognize and eventually understand. He will also learn better when spoken to occasionally in singsong tones.

Jack in the Box

- This fingerplay game develops your toddler's fine motor skills.
- Say the following rhyme, and do the accompanying motions.

  Jack in the box, Jack in the box (Make a fist with your right hand, and hide your thumb inside.)
  It's time to wake up and smile. (Knock on your fist with your other hand.)
  One, two, three, four (Keep knocking.)
  Out Jack pops from his little, round door.
  (Pop your thumb out from inside your fist.)

What brain research says

Hand and finger exercises stimulate brain growth. Researchers have confirmed the positive effects of fingerplays on the brain.

- Repeat the poem, and encourage your toddler to do the actions with you.

Fill It Up

- Locate an unbreakable container that has a relatively wide opening on top.
- Use solid wooden clothespins or other safe objects.
- Demonstrate for your little one how to drop the items into the container.
- Invite your little one to fill up the container, either by placing the items into the container or by standing up and attempting to drop them in.
- Point out the sounds as the objects drop: loud, soft, high, and low.

What brain research says

Young children need to develop muscle control and coordination so they are ready when they are older to do academic tasks such as writing.

Important Play

- As your toddler gets older, she is remembering more, able to stay focused for longer periods of time, and is interested in imitating you.
- Observe her play, and when the opportunity arises, add another dimension to what she is doing.
- If your toddler is pretending to talk on the phone, talk back to her as if you are someone else: "Hi, Samantha. This is Grandma. How are you today?"
- If your toddler is holding a block, pick up a second block, and put it on top of her block.
- Tell your toddler that you are putting the block *on* her block. Now take the block off. Other actions and words you can use are *in front of, behind,* and so on.
- If you see that your toddler is getting overly excited or is no longer interested in this game, introduce a slower-paced activity or let your child engage in independent play for a while.

What brain research says

Gently guiding your child to the next step stretches her brain capacity.

The Wonders of Music

- Listening to different types of music nurtures your toddler's self-esteem and encourages creativity, self-confidence, and curiosity.
- Try these ideas:
  - Play lullabies, and rock your baby in your arms.
  - Play marches, and hold your baby as you march around the room. You can even say the word *march* as you move.
  - Play soft and gentle music as you glide around the room with your little one.
  - Play fast music as you hold your baby on your lap facing you and clap his hands together quickly.

What brain research says

Music stimulates brain connections. A study from the University of California found that music trains the brain for higher forms of thinking. Researchers believe that music affects spatial-temporal reasoning (the ability to see part/whole relationships).

Saying Names

- This game develops a toddler's thinking skills.
- When a toddler is learning to talk, she likes to say her own name again and again. Sometimes she may call other people by her own name because she has not learned that a name relates to a particular person.
- To help toddlers learn that people and objects each have separate names, touch an object, such as a table.
- Take your toddler's hand, and put it on the table as you say the word *table*.
- Touch the table again, and say, "(child's name) is touching the table." As you say the word *table*, touch the table.
- Repeat this game by touching other objects in the room or parts of the child's body.
- Do this with other objects or with people the child knows.

What brain research says

Research shows that sensory experiences and social interactions with supportive adults develop thinking abilities.

Construction 101

- Provide your little one with blocks or other materials that can be stacked.
- Count or describe the items as your child stacks them.
- Encourage your child to keep stacking and building with the blocks.
- Eventually the structure will collapse, or your child will choose to knock it down.
- Talk to your child about what happens when the stack falls or is knocked down.

What brain research says

Fine and gross motor skills are necessary for many tasks. Eye-hand coordination is necessary for the development of these skills.

Follow the Leader

- By encouraging your toddler to copy you as you do different activities, you help him develop his observation and listening skills.
- If your little one is crawling, crawl to different parts of a room, and do silly activities.
- If your toddler is walking, do the same activities by walking or combining walking and crawling.
- Describe what you are doing. For example, say, "I am walking (or crawling) slowly around the chair."
- Here are a few ideas:

- Crawl or walk to the wall, and say, "Ta-da!"
- Crawl or walk to the door, and count to three.
- Walk in a circle, sit down, and say, "Chi, chi, boom!"

What brain research says

A child's brain thrives on feedback from the environment. It "wires" itself into a thinking and emotional organ based on its experiences.

Sing Out

- Enjoy singing with your toddler any time during the day—while you are in the car, waiting in line at the supermarket, or sitting in a doctor's office. Anytime is a good time to sing.
- Don't worry about singing in key or changing the words of a song. The important part is to enjoy the singing.
- The following are some suggestions for songs, although any song you know and love would be fine:

"Five Little Ducks"   "On Top of Spaghetti"
"Going to the Zoo"   "Skip to My Lou"
"I'm a Little Teapot"   "The Itsy, Bitsy Spider"
"If You're Happy, and   "This Old Man"
You Know It"

- Sing the song again, and add actions.
- Move your toddler's hands to help her clap, wave, or do any other motion. Or, do the action first, and then let your toddler do it.

What brain research says

The earlier a child is introduced to music, the more responsive she will be to music throughout her life, and the more her brain will develop as a result.

Story Time

- Story time develops a toddler's prereading skills and encourages him to love books and reading.
- Reading books to a toddler can be frustrating. It is important to realize that two to four minutes is about as long as your little one can sit still.
- Toddlers are interested in books with photos of children doing everyday things that are familiar to them, like eating, running, and sleeping.
- Books about saying hello and goodbye are also popular with this age.
- Simple rhymes and predictable text are also important criteria for a toddler book.
- To increase your child's interest in a book, substitute your child's name for the name of a child in the book.
- You can read anywhere and anytime—on a bed, at bathtime (using waterproof books, of course), on the floor, or in a swing.

What brain research says

Reading books aloud to children stimulates their imaginations and expands their understanding of the world. It helps children develop language and listening skills and prepares them to understand written words.

The Cuddle Game

- Cuddling with your toddler is a very important way to develop brain capacity and trust.
- In times of danger, cuddling is even more important.
- If your little one wanders where she is not allowed to go, pick her up and cuddle her while explaining, "You cannot go there because it is dangerous."
- She will understand by the tone of your voice that what she did is a no-no.
- By the way that you hold her as you say those words, she will also understand that you care for and want to protect her.

What brain research says

Young children fall in love with their parents; psychologists call this attachment. In the 1950s, British psychiatrist John Bowlby highlighted the importance of attachment. It remains an enduring theory of human development.

All Wrapped Up

- Have your little one lie down on the floor on an end of a blanket or beach towel. (Keep your child's head off of the blanket or beach towel.)
- Carefully help your child roll over and over as you wrap the blanket or beach towel around his body.
- Scoop up your wrapped-up child, and rock him back and forth while laughing and kissing his face.
- Reverse the process by carefully placing your child back down on the floor and slowly unrolling the blanket or beach towel.

What brain research says

Attachment and bonding are critical in the early years. The more nurtured, loved, cared for, and safe a child feels, the more firmly established his emotional well-being will be.

Everyone Sleeps

- Establishing a bedtime routine for your little one is very important.
- Locate a box or an appropriate piece of furniture to make an additional small bed in your child's room.
- Let your little one place a small doll or stuffed animal into the bed and cover it with a blanket.
- After your child has helped tuck in the doll or animal, she will be more ready for a nap or bedtime.

What brain research says

The brain seeks patterns to understand information. When the brain receives new information, it looks to previous patterns to help it understand this new information.

Everything Can Talk

- This game is a playful way to develop your child's language skills.
- Hold a favorite stuffed animal, such as a teddy bear, up to your ear as if you were listening to what it is saying. Tell your toddler that teddy says, "Let's play."
- Use a high-pitched voice when you say, "Let's play."
- Give the teddy to your toddler, and ask him what he thinks the teddy is saying.
- Continue playing the game by asking what different toys or objects in the room say. For example, a chair can say, "Soft."
- Always use a high-pitched voice when speaking for the toy or object.

What brain research says

Your toddler's brain is forging the pathways that will be used for the rest of his life. Connections that are used repeatedly will become permanent. Everything you do with your toddler—playing, talking, eating, walking, reading, cuddling, and singing—helps jump-start his brain. When you use your imagination with him, you help his brain to make "imagination pathways" of its own.

Chook, chook

- This fingerplay is a wonderful way to develop your child's fine motor skills. And it is lots of fun to do!
- Sit your toddler in your lap, and move her fingers to fit the rhyme.

Chook, chook, (Say this like a chicken would.)
Chook, chook, chook,
Good morning, Mrs. Hen.
How many chickens have you got?
Madam, I've got ten. (Hold up your child's 10 fingers.)
Four of them are yellow, (Put down four fingers on one hand; keep the thumb up.)
And four of them are brown, (Put down four fingers on the other hand; keep the thumb up.)
And two of them are speckled red, (Touch the thumb of each hand.)
The nicest in the town. (Kiss your child's two thumbs.)

What brain research says

Small muscle exercises like fingerplays stimulate brain growth. Researchers have confirmed the positive effects on the brain of simple hand and finger movements.

Bonjour and Buenos Dias

- Your toddler is the perfect age for exposure to the sounds of other languages.
- If you speak two languages, talk to your toddler in both languages.
- Start with simple words such as numbers, colors, and names of body parts.
- Even if you speak only English, try the following greetings in different languages:

  Hola (ō'-la)—Spanish
  Ciao (chow)—Italian
  Moshi moshi (mō'-she mō'-she)—Japanese
  Jambo (jahm'-bo)—Swahili
  Shalom (sha-lōm')—Hebrew
  Yassou (yah-soo')—Greek

- Listen to songs in another language. You will be amazed at how quickly your child will learn words in another language. Even if he isn't saying the words, his brain is sending all the right signals for the sounds of this language to be retained.
- If you know someone who speaks another language, visit with that person so your toddler can hear that person speak in that language.
- Read stories that incorporate words in languages other than your native tongue.

What brain research says

When a child hears the sounds of a language, neural links are formed in the brain, allowing the child to build vocabulary in that language. Recent brain research suggests that, ideally, exposure to a second language should begin at birth.

One Little Foot, I Love You

- Sit on the floor with your toddler in your lap.
- Lift up one of her feet, and chant the following:

    One little foot, I love you.
    One little foot, I love you.
    Shake it to the left. (Move your toddler's foot to the left.)
    Shake it to the right. (Move your toddler's foot to the right.)
    One little foot, I love you.

- Kiss your toddler's foot.
- Repeat the chant as long as your child is still enjoying the experience.
- Repeat the chant using different parts of the body

    One little hand…
    One little finger…
    One little head…

What brain research says

Between 12 and 18 months, a baby's emotions begin to develop, including the emotions that are closely connected with long-term memory. Toddlers need secure attachment with a sensitive, predictable primary caregiver. A feeling of security gradually becomes part of a toddler's sense of self, allowing her to venture further out into the world with confidence and enthusiasm.

37

The Cow Says, "Moo"

Moo

- Toddlers love animal sounds. Learning animal sounds is often the first step in beginning speech.
- Toddlers need to say as many sounds as they can. The more they talk, the more they will want to talk.
- Look through an animal picture book, and talk about the sounds that the animals make.
- Make an animal sound that your child will recognize, and ask him to show you a picture in the book of the animal that makes that sound.
- Add other sounds to your repertoire— a car engine, a fire engine siren, bird calls, and other sounds in your toddler's environment.
- Help your child become aware of the sounds around him.

What brain research says

The brain has an almost boundless capacity to store information. When the brain processes new information, it forms neural networks.

Brain Clapping

- Show your child different ways to clap her hands.

  - Hold the left palm faceup and the right palm facedown. Move the right palm so it claps on top of the left palm.
  - Reverse, holding the right palm and moving the left palm to clap on the right palm.
  - Clap her hands together behind her head.
  - Clap her hands together on the left side.
  - Clap her hands together on the right side.

- Sing your favorite songs as you clap different ways.

What brain research says

Doing one activity in many different ways makes the brain more alert and helps improve learning.

Motions for Songs

- The more actions you do when you sing songs, the more fun it is for your toddler.
- Make up actions to go with favorite songs. Here are some ideas:

  - "The Itsy, Bitsy Spider": Crawl the fingers of one hand up the arm of the other hand. Pretend raindrops are falling when you sing about rain falling.
  - "Twinkle, Twinkle, Little Star": Put your hands up in the air, and wiggle your fingers like twinkling stars.
  - "The Wheels on the Bus": Create an action for each verse. For example, move your hands in a circular motion for the first verse; move your arms back and forth for the verse about the wipers going swish, swish, swish; and pretend to be a horn for the verse about the horn going beep, beep, beep.

What brain research says

When you sing and clap or wave and move your arms up and down, you are using both sides of the brain.

Looking at Me

- Look into a mirror with your toddler.
- Let him watch his face as he does different actions.
- As he watches himself in the mirror, ask him to do the following:

  - Smile.
  - Stick out his tongue and inspect it.
  - Open and close his mouth.
  - Look at his teeth.

- Give him something to eat, and let him watch himself chew (with his mouth closed, of course!).
- This game helps him become more aware of himself and his abilities.

What brain research says

Social interactions with supportive adults help children develop thinking abilities.

Cat and Mouse

- Tell your toddler that you are a tiny little mouse and that she is a cat that is going to chase you.
- Tell her that the mouse says, "Squeak, squeak," and the cat says, "Meow, meow."
- Get down on the floor and say, "You can't catch me!" Start crawling quickly, and encourage your child to chase you.
- Crawl behind furniture, under tables, and into other rooms.
- When your child understands the game, switch roles.
- This is a wonderful way to develop your toddler's large motor skills.

What brain research says

Exercise forms and strengthens the neural bridges that are necessary for all learning, including the academic skills that your toddler will learn as she gets older.

Big Feet

- Bring out some large shoes, and let your toddler put them on and try to walk.
- This game is lots of fun. It can be quite a challenge for your child to keep his balance as he walks from one location to another!

What brain research says

Understanding how the body moves and where the body is in space helps develop self-awareness and self-control.

Words, Words, Words

- Cut out magazine pictures of objects that are familiar to your toddler, such as animals, babies, and food.
- Look at the pictures with your toddler, and talk about each picture.
- For example, point to a cow and say, "The cow is at the farm. 'Moo, moo,' says the cow."
- Now, ask your toddler what the cow says. If she doesn't respond, repeat what you said.
- Point to a baby, and say, "The baby is in the cradle. The baby says, 'Waa, waa.'" Then ask your toddler what the baby says.
- Talk about a picture that your child has already seen, then add a new picture.
- Let your child choose one of the pictures and tell you about it, or make up a short, simple story about one of the pictures for your toddler.

What brain research says

Children learn a language by hearing words over and over. That's why the more you talk to children, the better.

Someone Special

- Develop your toddler's listening skills by saying the following poem:

  I know someone very special.
  Do you know who?
  I'll turn around and turn
  around. (Turn around.)
  And then I'll point to you!
  (Point to your child.)
  by Jackie Silberg

- Ask your child to turn around as you say the poem.
- Repeat the poem, and change the action. Instead of turning around, you can jump up and down, clap your hands, fly like a bird, or any other action that you and your child enjoy.
- This game develops your child's listening skills because he must listen to know what to do.

What brain research says

When children have a nurturing environment early in life, their ability to learn is enhanced, and they adjust more easily to new situations.

Working Together

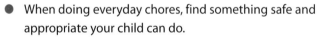

- When doing everyday chores, find something safe and appropriate your child can do.
- Your toddler can practice simple sorting skills with the laundry. For example, she can find all the socks, then all the shirts, and so on.
- Provide containers or bags so your child can help pick up her toys or other objects.
- Encourage your child by telling her how helpful it is when you work together.

What brain research says

Working together in a playful way creates a positive feeling of attachment and a healthy self-concept.

Let's Talk

- Talking with your toddler develops his language skills.
- Choose a subject that he is interested in. It might be about his toys, grandparents, friends, or pets.
- Add descriptive words as you talk about a particular subject. For example, say to a toy rabbit, "I like this bunny rabbit. It feels soft and cuddly."
- As you say these words, cuddle the toy and stroke it.
- Give the bunny rabbit to your toddler. Repeat the words, and encourage him to cuddle and stroke the rabbit.
- Think of other words that you can use to describe the bunny rabbit.
- The words *soft* and *cuddly* can apply to other toys.
- Soon these descriptive words will become a part of your toddler's vocabulary.

What brain research says

Early experiences are critical. When a child reaches school-age, his learning is building on the foundation laid down in the first three years.

Touch the Animals

- Go on a trip to a farm or petting zoo that offers interaction with the animals.
- As you look at, touch, pet, hold, and listen to the animals, talk to your toddler about everything that is going on around her.
- Use lots of language about the animals.
- Ask your child to name the animals that she recognizes from books.
- Listen for the animal sounds, and invite your child to imitate the sounds she hears.

What brain research says

The brain works best in a state of high challenge and low threat. Safe, new, and fun experiences strengthen neural connections.

125 Brain Games for Toddlers and Twos

Let's Make Music

- Toddlers respond best to music when they experience it actively.
- Play games that involve rocking, tapping, clapping, and moving.
- Pick three familiar songs, and assign a particular movement to each one. For example:

  - "The Itsy, Bitsy Spider"— Use the actions that go with the song.
  - "The Wheels on the Bus"—Sit your toddler in your lap, and bounce your legs while holding him at the waist.
  - "Twinkle, Twinkle, Little Star"—Clap your hands as you march around the room together.

- Choose one of the actions, and ask your toddler sing the song with you.
- Once he is familiar with the chosen actions, you can do two different things:

  - Do an action, and ask him if he can tell you what song it is.
  - Ask him to choose the action, and then you can sing the song together.

What brain research says

Musical games that combine rhythmic movement with singing develop a child's memory skills.

The Classics

- Listening to classical music is a wonderful activity to share with your toddler.
- Select some music that is fast and some that is slow.
- Dance to the music, and encourage your toddler to join you.
- Music such as "Flight of the Bumblebee" by Nikolai Rimsky-Korsakov is a good choice, because it is fast and you can pretend to be a bee buzzing around the room.
- Classical music that is soft and gentle will relax your child and is excellent to play during nap time.
- Here are a few suggestions for classical music to use:

  - "The Blue Danube" (Johann Strauss II)—infectious waltz music to dance to
  - *Carnival of the Animals* (Camille Saint-Saëns)—instruments imitate animals
  - "Clair de Lune" (Claude Debussy)—music that describes moonlight
  - *The Nutcracker* (Pyotr Ilich Tchaikovsky)—excellent for acting out
  - "William Tell Overture" (Gioachino Rossini)—familiar, lively music

What brain research says

When listening to classical music, the brain circuits used for mathematics are strengthened. Listening to music also enhances the neural pathways used for complex reasoning tasks.

Hippity Hoppity

- Develop your toddler's language skills by saying the following poem and doing the actions.

  Hippity hoppity, hippity hoppity, (Jump like a bunny rabbit.)
  Hippity hoppity, stop. (Stop jumping.)
  I'm so tired. I'm so tired. (Yawn.)
  I think I'm going to flop. (Fall down on the ground.)
  by Jackie Silberg

- When you have stopped hopping, ask your child why the bunny rabbit was so tired.
- Suggest things the rabbit might have seen while it was hopping around.
- Talk about the places the rabbit might have gone—into your yard, down the block, behind a bush, or into a garden.
- Give your child the words, and before you know it, she will be making up her own poem.

What brain research says

The number of words a child hears in the first three years of life has a direct effect on the size of her adult vocabulary.

In My Little Corner of the World

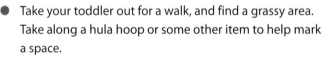

- Take your toddler out for a walk, and find a grassy area. Take along a hula hoop or some other item to help mark a space.
- Get down on the grass together, and take a look at all the things inside the marked space.
- Invite your little one to notice bugs, the grass, leaves, twigs, stones, and any other thing inside the hoop.
- Talk to your child about the things he sees, touches, and possibly smells.

What brain research says

Free exploration, choice, and discovery are keys to making neural connections, as well as to strengthening the ability to focus on a task and to fostering self-control.

Listen to the Sound

- Take your toddler outside.
- Help her become aware of the wonderful sounds of the outdoors.
- Start listening for birds. When you hear a bird call, try to copy the sound. Tell your child that you are making the "birdie sound."
- If you continue making the bird sound, your child will become aware of the sound and may try to duplicate it.
- Add new sounds, such as the wind blowing or crickets chirping.
- Listen for other sounds in your environment, such as cars, motorcycles, and trains.

What brain research says

Expose your little one to a variety of sensory stimuli—colors, music, language, natural and mechanical sounds, touch experiences, smells, tastes—to ensure that, when she is an adult, she will be both flexible and focused.

Special Day Together

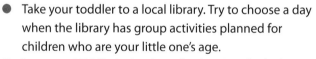

- Take your toddler to a local library. Try to choose a day when the library has group activities planned for children who are your little one's age.
- Let your child find a book to check out and take home.
- Look for a variety of play activities that are available in the library to extend the time.
- Revisit the library often so your toddler knows a great place and resource to find new and interesting books.

What brain research says

The brain seeks patterns to establish new neural pathways. Routines and repeated interactions become the norm and standard for lifelong practice.

Important Accents

- Saying nursery rhymes is a wonderful way to develop language and prereading skills.
- Try this game with rhymes that your toddler knows.
- Say the rhyme, any rhyme, and put an accent on the first syllable of each word.
- Any rhyme will do, but the following work well:

  - "London Bridge Is Falling Down"
  - "Mary Had a Little Lamb"
  - "Twinkle, Twinkle, Little Star"

- Try some of your favorite rhymes.

What brain research says

Scientists have found that young children have a clear preference for words with first-syllable accents.

Food Fun

- Cooking or preparing simple foods with young children can be a total learning experience as well as lots of fun.
- Cooking or preparing food with toddlers can include the experiences of feeling the textures, smelling the food, talking about shapes and sizes, and discussing colors.
- Here is a simple cooking activity to do with your toddler:

  - Cut a banana into small pieces.
  - Put each banana piece on a spoon.
  - Dip each banana piece in a small glass of orange juice.
  - Roll the banana pieces in coconut.
  - Eat!

What brain research says

By providing warm, responsive care, you strengthen the connections that allow your child to cope with difficult moments.

Songs and Pics

- Fill an unbreakable, widemouthed jar with pictures that represent familiar songs. For example, use a picture of a bus for "The Wheels on the Bus."
- Look through magazines and catalogs with your little one to find pictures that represent songs he knows.
- Let your child choose a picture from the jar, and sing the song together.
- Here are some ideas:

  - Bells—"Jingle Bells"
  - Birthday cake—"Happy Birthday" (This will be a favorite.)
  - Bus—"The Wheels on the Bus"
  - Lamb—"Mary Had a Little Lamb"
  - Rowboat—"Row, Row, Row Your Boat"
  - Sky with stars—"Twinkle, Twinkle, Little Star"
  - Tea kettle—"I'm a Little Teapot"

What brain research says

Brain research shows that music and singing activates brain activity that stimulates new learning and helps in memory processes. Singing and music encourage the use of many senses, and this also helps in learning and developing language skills. Music activities use both hemispheres in the brain, which will prepare the brain for more difficult tasks in the future.

Making Jewelry

- Take a cardboard tube from the center of a paper towel roll.
- Tape the cardboard tube to a table to stabilize it so your toddler can decorate it with crayons. Move the cardboard tube from time to time until it is completely decorated with crayons.
- Cut it up into small sections, and string the pieces onto a piece of yarn.
- Put the necklace on your child so she can proudly wear her own creation. **Safety Note**: Whenever she wears the necklace, take special care so there the necklace does not pose a choking hazard.

What brain research says

The brain learns and makes connections between neurons through play.

Clap Your Hands

- Sing the following very slowly to the tune of "Row, Row, Row Your Boat."

  Clap, clap, clap your hands
  Slowly every day. (Clap your hands slowly.)
  Merrily, merrily, merrily, merrily,
  (Keep clapping.)
  Then we shout, "Hooray!" (Jump up and down, and shout *"H-o-o-ray"* slowly.)

- Sing this verse faster.

  Clap, clap, clap your hands
  Faster every day. (Clap your hands faster.)
  Merrily, merrily, merrily, merrily,
  Then we shout, "Hooray!"
  by Jackie Silberg

- Sing this song with different actions. Always do the actions slowly at first, then speed them up. When children repeat actions at different speeds, they begin to internalize the concepts.
- Other actions to try include rolling your hands, shaking your hands, waving your hands, stamping your feet, and shaking your hips.

What brain research says

Early musical experiences increase and enhance spatial-temporal reasoning, which advances the learning of mathematical concepts.

Funky Sounds

- Locate several types of containers with tight-fitting lids.
- Fill each container with a different material, such as sand, buttons, bells, stones, beads, birdseed, and so on.
- Securely attach the lids with superglue, then cover the edges with tape. You can decorate the outside of the containers if you like.
- Give your toddler the opportunity to shake and make some noise with each container. You may want to leave one container empty just for fun.
- Talk to your child about the different sounds he hears when he shakes the containers.

What brain research says

Auditory (sound) discrimination is the first step toward being able to discriminate among letter sounds—a reading skill.

Learning with Play

- Select several objects such as a hairbrush, a spoon, and a cup that your toddler is familiar with and uses regularly.
- Put the objects on the floor.
- Sit in front of the objects.
- Pick up one object, such as the hairbrush, and pretend to brush your hair.
- Pick up each object, and pretend to use it.
- Ask your toddler to pick up one of the objects and show how she would use it.
- This is a great game to develop your toddler's thinking skills and help her imagine many things to do with the same object, such as using a cup for drinking and for pouring.

What brain research says

Brain research underscores what educators have long known: Early social and emotional experiences are the seeds of human intelligence. Developing the brain's neural circuits allows those seeds to grow.

Oh, My Goodness! Oh, My Gracious!

- To give your child a sense of security and safety, say the following:

  Oh, my goodness,
  Oh, my gracious,
  Look who's here! Look who's here!
  Oh, my goodness,
  Oh, my gracious,
  It's my favorite (child's name)*!*

- Hold your child close, and give him a big hug.
- Repeat the poem again; when you hug your child, hold him high in the air, and then bring him down for a big kiss.
- Try rocking him or slowly spinning him around or moving him in any other loving way.
- Your little one will absolutely love this!

What brain research says

When children receive warm, responsive care, they are more likely to feel safe and secure and will be able to build attachments to others.

I'm in the Band

- Create a simple horn by decorating a cardboard tube with construction paper, markers, stickers, or other materials.

  - Place a square of waxed paper over one end of the tube, and attach it with a rubber band.
  - Show your toddler how to hum.
  - Put the tube up to your mouth, and hum into the open end so your little one can hear the unique sound.
  - Encourage your child to hum into the horn.

- If humming is too challenging, encourage your child to sing or make other types of noises in the tube. **Safety Note:** Rubber bands can pose a choking hazard.

What brain research says

Music—creating it, listening to it, or performing it—creates unique brain connections that contribute to the understanding of math concepts, spatial reasoning, and other complex ideas.

Dress-Up

- Toddlers love to play dress-up. As you describe and talk about the various clothes, you are developing her language and vocabulary skills.
- Gather together all kinds of clothing—hats, scarves, shoes, gloves, or whatever you think that your toddler would enjoy.
- Put on one of the hats, and say, "How do you do, (child's name)?"
- Put on a glove, and say, "Oh, this feels so smooth."
- Ask your child to pick an article of clothing. If necessary, help her talk about the clothing by providing one or two words that describe it.
- Soon, a conversation will develop, and the language will flow.

What brain research says

The more an adult talks to a child, the larger the child's vocabulary will be by the age of two.

I Can Do It Myself

- Find some clothing or other objects with easy-to-fasten buttons, zippers, snaps, buckles, hooks, and so on. You could also include pocketbooks, wallets, and backpacks.
- Fill a basket or bag with the items, and encourage your little one to start figuring out how to open and close each item.
- Demonstrate how each works.
- Encourage your child each time he is successful by saying, "You did it! You pulled up the zipper," or "Wow! You got that snap together."

What brain research says

Learning new skills fosters your child's self-confidence, mental health, and resiliency.

Fly, Little Bird

- Stand and face your toddler. Take her hands in yours.
- While holding hands, walk around in a circle, and chant or say the following:

  Fly, little bird, through the window.
  (Pretend to fly.)
  Fly, little bird, through the door. (Pretend to fly.)
  Fly, little bird, through the window.
  Fly, and touch the chair.

- On the line "Fly, and touch the chair," pretend to fly and touch a chair (or another object in the room). Ask your toddler to do the same thing.
- Fly and touch something different.
- What a fun way to teach vocabulary!

What brain research says

From its beginnings at birth to trillions of connections by age three, scientists tell us the brain grows at an unparalleled rate during the early years.

On the Road Again

- Use masking tape, painter's tape, or another type of tape to create a path for vehicles or walking. **Hint**: Apply tape to an inconspicuous area first, to test how the tape will react to your carpet or flooring.
- Encourage your child to roll a car or truck along the path.
- The path can also be used to practice walking and balancing on a line.
- Increase the complexity, direction, or length of the "highway" as appropriate for your child.

What brain research says

Keeping one's balance and staying on a line are complex skills that exercise many parts of the brain.

Sink or Float

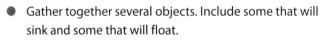

- Gather together several objects. Include some that will sink and some that will float.
- Suggestions include sponges, soap, empty containers, full containers, floating toys, and small toys that will not be damaged by the water.
- Fill a dishpan or bucket with a few inches of water. **Safety Note**: Never leave a child unsupervised around water.
- Put one item at a time in the water.
- After each item, use the words *sink* or *float* to describe what each item does.
- After you have tried each object individually, start again.
- This time, before you put an item into the water, ask your toddler, "Do you think it will float or sink?"
- Soon your toddler will be looking for other items to see if they will sink or float.

What brain research says

Problem solving leads to new understanding. A playful, nonthreatening atmosphere supports brain development.

Rhythm Fun

- Sit on the floor with your child, and give him a rhythm stick or a wooden spoon.

- Tap a particular rhythm. For example, hit the stick two times and then stop. Count as you hit the stick, "One, two…"

- If your little one cannot tap a distinct rhythm, hold his hand, and hit the stick on the floor as you count.

- Sing a song, and tap your stick on the floor to the rhythm of the song. Encourage your child to copy you.

- Continue to play this game as you experiment with tapping different rhythms with the stick.

- Once your child understands how to control the stick, give him directions, and see if he can follow along.

  - Tap your stick fast.
  - Tap your stick slowly.
  - Tap your stick loudly.
  - Tap your stick softly.

- This game will teach your child to become more aware of rhythm.

What brain research says

Experiencing rhythmic patterns and practicing fine muscle control create key neural circuits in your toddler's developing brain.

Baster Blaster

- You will need two unbreakable containers.
- Fill one unbreakable container with a few inches of water. Add a few drops of food coloring to the water.
- Show your toddler how to use a baster, by squeezing and releasing the bulb and allowing the colored water in the bowl to rise up in the baster.
- Help your toddler move the water-filled baster to another empty unbreakable container, squeeze the baster, and let the water begin to fill up the other container.
- Let your little one continue the process of transferring the water from one container to another.
- This is a great idea to try outdoors on a warm day.

What brain research says

Fine motor development in very young children is key to skills that your child will need as she gets older, such as writing.

Spin, Spin, Little Top

- Show your child a top, and let him watch it spin.
- Demonstrate how to spin like a top, and ask him to copy you.
- Say the following, and spin like tops:

*Spin, spin, little top
Spinning 'round and 'round.
Spin, spin, little top
Falling slowly to the ground.*

- Once your toddler understands the game, start to spin slowly and then faster and faster.
- Slow down before you hit the ground.

What brain research says

Repeating motor skills over and over strengthens the neural circuits that go from the brain's thinking areas to the motor areas and out to the nerves that move muscles.

Old MacDonald

- Toddlers enjoy singing "Old MacDonald Had a Farm" because they love to make the animal sounds.
- Try this new version of the song:

    Old MacDonald had a cold, E, I, E, I, O.
    And with his cold he had a cough, E, I, E, I, O.

- Add sounds you might make when you have a cold.
- Old MacDonald could also have a yard, a house, a bookstore, and so on. Changing the words develops your child's vocabulary.
- For a challenge, sing the original song as a sequential song, repeating each animal mentioned at the end of each verse.

What brain research says

A neurological scan of a child who is singing nursery rhymes or doing counting games would show sections of her brain literally glowing with activity.

Daily Music

- Sing throughout the day to your toddler.
- Make up songs about what you are doing in addition to singing your regular favorite songs.
- Smile when you sing, and vary your voice as you sing.
- Encourage your little one to join you.
- Singing introduces words, rhymes, rhythms, melody, and many sounds.

What brain research says

Research indicates that exposure to music has numerous benefits for a child's development. Music promotes language acquisition, listening skills, memory, and motor skills. Songs introduce new words, often ones that rhyme or repeat, which makes them easy to learn.

Patterns with Blocks

- Show your toddler how he can make simple patterns with blocks.
- See if he can copy you. Help him if he needs it.
- For example, put three blocks in a row. As you do it, tell him what you are doing, and count each block as you put it down.
- Count again as he tries to copy you. Help him if necessary.
- The following are some patterns that you can try:

  - Three blocks on the bottom and one on top in the middle
  - Two blocks, one on top of the other

- Encourage your child to make different patterns and shapes with the blocks while you copy him.

What brain research says

Creative ideas occur when the brain is in a relaxed state. Our minds are open to combining what we already know with new information. Our brains are then able to generate new thoughts and ideas.

Here Comes the Ball

- Sit on the floor facing your toddler, with your legs apart and her toes touching yours.
- Say to her, "I will roll the ball to you." Roll the ball slowly to her.
- When she catches the ball, praise her, and ask her to roll it back.
- Make a game of it by counting to three and rolling on three. Encourage your toddler to count with you.
- Make up other fun words for rolling the ball back and forth. For example, say, "Hinky Dinky Doo!" Roll the ball on *doo*.
- This game will build arm muscle strength and eye-hand coordination.

What brain research says

Even the simplest game introduces new skills and ideas, as neural pathways multiply.

Look at Yourself

- This is a wonderful game to help your child think about the different parts of his body and to enhance his observation skills.

- Say to your two-year-old, "If you are wearing shoes, jump up and down."

- Help your child by asking, "Do you have on shoes? Show me where they are."

- Point to his shoes, and ask him to jump up and down. You might need to demonstrate how to jump.

- Each time you ask your child about himself, follow up by pointing to that part of his body and showing him how to do the action.

- Here are other ideas:

  - If you are wearing socks, twist back and forth.
    - If you are wearing a shirt, clap your hands.
      - If you are wearing pants, shake your head up and down.

- Once you have played this game a few times, your child may be able to do the actions without your help.

What brain research says

Families and educators have a golden opportunity to develop children's brains. A rich environment filled with loving challenges sets the stage for the future.

Whispering

- Two-year-olds are fascinated by whispering and are very proud when they can do it.
- Whispering helps a child learn to modulate her voice, an important aspect of sound awareness. It also takes a lot of concentration.
- Whisper something to your two-year-old, such as, "Let's clap our hands."
- Ask your two-year-old to whisper something back to you.
- Keep whispering to each other until your two-year-old understands how to make her voice very soft.

What brain research says

Each time a child is stimulated to think, either new neural pathways are formed or existing ones are strengthened.

Shake It All About

- Play this game with a stuffed animal or doll that has hands and feet.
- Sit on the floor with your two-year-old, and show him how to take the stuffed animal's arms and shake them up and down.
- Give the stuffed animal to your child, and let him try it.
- Think of all the things that you can do with your stuffed animal.
- Here are some ideas:

- Wave its hand.
- Clap its hands.
- Move its legs up and down.
- Clap its feet together.
- Make it throw a kiss.

- Ask your two-year-old for his ideas.

What brain research says

Positive early experiences and interactions have a significant impact on a child's emotional development.

Learning Rhymes

- Two-year-olds are like sponges. They hear something once and immediately begin to absorb it, especially if it involves actions.

- An interesting way to say nursery rhymes is to accent the last word of each line and do an action at the same time. This will help your child memorize the rhyme.

- Here is an example. Remember to accent the last word.

Hickory, dickory, DOCK (Move your fingers in a climbing motion.)
The mouse ran up the CLOCK. (Climb your fingers up again.)
The clock struck ONE, (Hold up one finger.)
The mouse did RUN. (Move the one finger downward.)
Hickory, dickory, DOCK. (Clap your hands on the word *dock*.)

What brain research says

Memory is learning that "sticks." When your child learns something, new synapses form or old synapses are strengthened, creating a memory of the experience or what the child learned.

Free Like the Wind

- It feels wonderful to hold a scarf and move freely to music. Doing this will give your child a sense of balance and control.
- Play some instrumental music as you and your child dance with scarves.
- Swoop the scarf high into the air and then low to the ground.
- Hold the scarf out as you turn in a circle.
  - You and your child can each hold one end of the scarf and dance together.
    - Whatever you do, your child will copy you.
    - This is a very creative game, and your child will want to play it again and again.

What brain research says

A child's capacity to learn and thrive in a variety of settings depends on the interplay between nature (her genetic endowment) and nurture (the kind of care, stimulation, and teaching she receives).

Smelly Times

- Help your child explore the way different things smell.
- Select things two things that have a distinctive smell and that are familiar to your child. A few suggestions include an orange, bath soap, and bananas.
- Show your child the two items, and let him smell them.
- Tell your child to close his eyes.
- Place one of the items near your child, and ask him to identify the item.

What brain research says

Playful interactions with concepts and ideas, created in a supportive environment, help children remember the concepts and ideas.

The Fruit Story

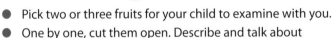

● Pick two or three fruits for your child to examine with you.

● One by one, cut them open. Describe and talk about what's inside. Does it have seeds, a core, or segments? What else do you notice about the fruit?

● Tell a story about the fruit, using your own words. The following is an example:

Once upon a time there was an apple that came to play with Billy. "Hi, Billy, I'm glad to be here, but I am a bit lonely. Could we invite another fruit to come over and play?"

"Okay," said Billy. "I'll call an orange."

Billy dialed the phone and said, "Hello, Orange. Would you like to come over to play?"

What brain research says

The plasticity of the brain, its ability to rewire itself, is what makes it so easy for children to learn language. The more words young children hear, the more connections their brains make.

● Let your child suggest another fruit to call. With each new fruit, examine it, talk about it, and of course, taste it.

I Can Help

- Involve your child in simple, age-appropriate jobs.
- One fun activity to do together is to give a pet a bath.
- Cleaning up, putting things away, wiping a table, and getting something for a sibling all draw upon a young child's desire to be social.
- Always tell your child that what she did was helpful, and remember to say, "Thank you!"

What brain research says

Socialization is key to healthy brain development because it creates bonds that make children comfortable enough to explore their environment. When they do, neurons in the brain are being stimulated to form new connections.

Sweet Little Bunny

- Play this game using your two-year-old's favorite stuffed animal. Change the name of "bunny" to the animal you are using.
- Say the following poem, and do the actions:

Sweet little bunny
Hopping on the ground. (Hold the bunny; make it hop up and down.)
Sweet little bunny
  Looking all around. (Turn the bunny around.)
   Look up high. (Hold the bunny high in the air.)
    Look down low. (Bring the bunny down to the ground.)
    Run, run, run. (Run with the bunny.)
    Oh, oh, oh,
    Sweet little bunny,
    Where did you go? (Hide the bunny behind your back.)

What brain research says

Scientists have found that your relationship with your child affects his brain in many ways. Gentle, loving fun combined with responsive language creates an atmosphere in which learning can thrive.

Up Close and Personal

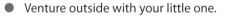

- Venture outside with your little one.
- Take along two unbreakable magnifying glasses, one for you and one for your child.
- Find a rock or log that is likely to have something interesting underneath it.
- Turn over the rock or log, and look for bugs, creatures, or objects.
- Give your child a magnifying glass so she can get a closer look at what is under the log or rock.
- If you take along an extra jar or large ziplock bag, you may able to bring home some of the more interesting finds and examine them again.
- After you have studied any living creature, release it outdoors.

What brain research says

New experiences encourage the development of higher-order thought processes.

Mirror, Mirror

- Sit on the floor with your child.
- Hold an unbreakable mirror in your hand, and say the following rhyme in a happy-sounding voice:

  Hello, mirror, what do you see?
  I see a happy face looking at me.

- Smile and make a happy face.
- Give the mirror to your child, and say the poem again. Ask him to make a happy face.
- Continue making different faces into the mirror. Demonstrate the face, and then let your child copy you.
- Other emotions to express are sad, grouchy, sleepy, angry, silly, and surprised.
- Make up a story using the different facial expressions that you have talked about. When you use words such as *happy*, *silly*, *sad*, and *angry*, express that emotion with your voice as well.

What brain research says

Children remember experiences that have an emotional component.

Paintbrushes

- Cut sponges into different shapes.
- Encourage your child to take the sponge shapes, dip them in nontoxic tempera paint, and print with them on a large piece of paper.
- Use other nontraditional materials for painting. A few ideas include feathers, an old toothbrush, pieces of balled-up paper towels, spools, and of course, fingers! Let your imagination guide you.

What brain research says

Encourage your child's creativity and imagination, which will develop her abstract thinking and problem-solving skills.

Looking at Trees

- Take your two-year-old for a walk outside. Go to a park or area where there are different kinds of trees.
- Find two or three freshly fallen leaves, and look at them with your child.
- Examine the sizes, shapes, and colors of the leaves; how the leaves feel; and how the leaves smell.
- Bring the leaves home, and dry or press them. When the leaves are dry, put them into a scrapbook to look at with your two-year-old.

What brain research says

Learning to see differences among similar objects develops the skills needed to recognize the alphabet.

Playing with Bubbles

- Blowing bubbles is a lovely game to play with two-year-olds. They will enjoy chasing bubbles, blowing them, and popping them.
- After a few experiences of exploring bubbles, ask your two-year-old some questions about the bubbles:

  - Are they all the same size?
  - What happens if you blow hard? (Do this with him.)
  - What happens if you blow softly? (Do this with him.)
  - What color are the bubbles?
  - Are all of the bubbles the same shape?
  - What happens if you touch a bubble?

- Pretend to be bubbles floating in the air. When your two-year-old touches you, say, "Pop!" and fall down.

What brain research says

Early experiences have a dramatic effect on the formation of brain synapses. The brain operates on the "use it or lose it" principle. Only those connections and pathways that are frequently used are retained. When children are in play mode, their brains are functioning at an optimal level.

Snack Time

- Let your little one help make a healthy snack.
- Choose from one of the following ideas, or create your own:

  - Fill an ice-cream cone with your favorite yogurt.
  - Dip graham cracker sticks in applesauce, pudding, or yogurt.
  - Roll banana slices in wheat germ and then in honey.

What brain research says

Challenging activities in a loving environment create optimal learning experiences.

My Little Bird

- Say the following poem, and do the actions to enhance your child's feeling of security:

Here is a nest
All warm inside
Where my little bird
Can safely hide. (Wrap your arms around your child, and hold her closely.)

Here is a nest
All hidden away
Where my little bird
Can sing and play. (Give your child a toy.)

Here is a nest
All cozy and deep
Where my little bird
Can go to sleep. (Rock your little one gently, and pretend to go to sleep.)

What brain research says

Children's brains are biologically "wired" to form strong emotional attachments between young children and their parents or caregivers.

Taking Turns

- Adults often get upset when their little ones don't want to share. Sharing is a very difficult concept for toddlers and two-year-olds.

- Taking turns is an easier way to begin to understand the concept of sharing.

- Give your child one of his favorite toys, and talk about the toy, including how colorful it is and how nice it feels.

- Take another toy for yourself, and describe it positively.

- Play with your toy, and ask your child to play with his toy, too.

- After a period of time, give your toy to your child, and ask to play with his toy.

- If this does not work the first time, try again later.

- The trust that your child has in you will encourage him to take turns.

What brain research says

Social skills are learned behaviors. To learn what to expect as a response or interaction in a particular situation, a child must practice the situation numerous times, preferably in a playful context.

Telling Stories

- Make up a story using your child's name: "Once upon a time there was a little girl named Maria."
- In the story, use two or three words that are repeated over and over. Encourage your child to say these words with you.
- For example, the story could be about "Maria" going to the park. Each time she sees something at the park that she recognizes, she says, "Hip, hip, hooray! Fun today."
- The following is an example of a story:

  Once upon a time there was a little girl named Maria. Maria loved to go to the park to see and do wonderful things. When she saw the flowers, she said, "Hip, hip, hooray! Fun today."

  Maria sat down on the soft, green grass and saw a little insect crawling by. She said, "Hip, hip, hooray! Fun today."

- Shorten or lengthen the story, depending on your child's interests and attention span.

What brain research says

Brain cells are "turned on," new connections are made, and existing connections are strengthened by experiences with stories.

Making Connections

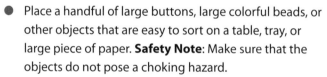

- Place a handful of large buttons, large colorful beads, or other objects that are easy to sort on a table, tray, or large piece of paper. **Safety Note:** Make sure that the objects do not pose a choking hazard.
- Encourage your child to find things that look alike or have similar characteristics.
- Let your child choose how he wishes to group things together—by size, shape, color, or another characteristic that makes sense to him.
- Talk about how many items your child put together. Count the items one by one.

What brain research says

The brain is a pattern-seeking organ. Neural connections are more readily made when new information can be attached to prior knowledge.

Jack Be Nimble

● Hold your child around the waist as you say the following popular nursery rhyme. Your child should be barefoot.

Jack be nimble.
Jack be quick. (Bounce your child while holding her around the waist.)
Jack jumped over the candlestick. (Bounce your child again.)
Jack jumped up high. (Hold your child high in the air.)
Jack jumped down low. (Bend down to the ground.)
Jack jumped over and burned his toe. (Say, "Oowww," and kiss your child's toe.)

What brain research says

Warm, everyday interactions like cuddling and singing will prepare children for learning throughout life.

Can You Do It, Too?

- Pretend to use an imaginary object, and tell your child what you are doing.
- For example, pretend to drink some milk.
- Say, "I am drinking some milk."
- Ask your two-year-old, "Can you do it, too?"
- Continue acting out simple activities that your child knows, such as the following:

  - Throw a ball.
  - Brush your teeth.
    - Wash your face.
    - Brush your hair.

What brain research says

At no other stage of life does the brain master so many activities with such ease.

- Always ask, "Can you do it, too?" after you do a pretend action.
- This kind of game develops your child's thinking and communication skills as well as his imagination.

Match Game

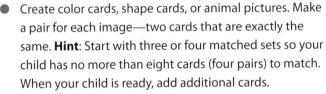

- Create color cards, shape cards, or animal pictures. Make a pair for each image—two cards that are exactly the same. **Hint**: Start with three or four matched sets so your child has no more than eight cards (four pairs) to match. When your child is ready, add additional cards.
- Turn the cards over in a random fashion.
- Encourage your child to turn over a card and name the color, shape, or animal.
- Have your child turn over another card, and see if it matches the first one overturned.
- If the cards do not match, place them back down in the same position and facedown.
- When two cards are found that match, let your child keep the pair.
- Continue until all the cards have been matched.

What brain research says

Trial and error in a loving environment fosters problem-solving skills.

Bump Ditty

- Take your two-year-old's favorite doll or stuffed animal.
- Ask her to touch the different parts of the doll's body. For example, say, "Show me teddy's head," or "Show me teddy's toes."
- Chant, say, or sing the following as you tap the teddy bear on its head with your index finger. Make up any melody.

Take your finger, and go like this:
Bump ditty, bump ditty, bump, bump, bump.

- Repeat the words as you tap the teddy's head with your child's finger.
- Say the rhyme again as you tap the teddy's nose or toe or knee.
- The repeating of the word *bump* is a very good rhythmic exercise.

What brain research says

Musical experiences integrate different skills simultaneously, thereby developing multiple brain connections.

Repeating

- Play a game with your two-year-old where you repeat the last word of a sentence three times.

  - Would you like some toast, toast, toast?
  - Can I brush your hair, hair, hair?
  - Let's play with toys, toys, toys.

- As you say the repeated word, accent the word the first time.
- Encourage your two-year-old to make up his own sentences and repeat them.

What brain research says

Children learn language by hearing words repeated over and over. Playing with words adds another dimension to the experience.

Fly with Me

- Take a trip to a local airport.
- Walk around the areas that are open to the public. If the airport has a tram, moving walkways, or even a play area, let your child explore the equipment.
- Talk to your child about what she sees—the planes, the restaurants, the ticket counters, the baggage claim area, escalators, or anything else that you notice.

What brain research says

Reinforce vocabulary with real experiences whenever possible. This offers your child the chance to see things firsthand and to say what she thinks about these new experiences.

Working at the Car Wash

- Fill a plastic tub or other large container with water and some soap solution. **Safety Note**: Never leave a child unattended around water.
- Ask your child to gather his cars, trucks, and other toys that move.
- Provide small sponges and clean towels.
- Encourage your child to wash each toy.
- Emphasize the name of the part of the vehicle or toy that is being washed—hood, trunk, window, door, back, front, top, bottom, and so on.
- Place the items in a sunny spot to dry.

What brain research says

Language and play work together to solidify concepts.

Rainbow Shopping

- Good nutrition is essential for brain development and function. Without it, children are unable to pay attention.
- Look at pictures of rainbows with your two-year-old, and name the different colors.
- Look in the kitchen for fruits and vegetables that match the rainbow colors.
- Try one or two of the fruits and vegetables each day. Find ways to let your child participate in the preparation of the fruits and vegetables.

What brain research says

When children eat healthy foods, the brain chemical serotonin (the "feel-good chemical") is released, and attention span is increased.

Wake Up Your Brain

- Play this game in the morning with your two-year-old.
- Lie down on the floor next to one another.
- Ask your two-year-old to copy your motions.
- Put one leg in the air, and show your two-year-old how to wiggle her toes. This will activate the nerves that stimulate the brain and other internal organs.
- Say the following poem as you do this exercise:

    Good morning, little toes,
    Wiggle, wiggle, wiggle. (Wiggle your toes.)
    How are you today?
    Wiggle, wiggle, wiggle. (Wiggle your toes.)
    It's time to put your shoes on,
    Wiggle, wiggle, wiggle. (Wiggle your toes.)
    And then we'll go and play,
    Wiggle, wiggle, wiggle. (Wiggle your toes.)

- Repeat this with your other leg.
- You can also play this game with additional parts of the body.

What brain research says

Physical activity enhances brain function through providing more oxygen to the brain.

The Sequence Game

- Sequencing is an important prereading skill.
- Sequencing means doing a series of things in a certain order or pattern. It also means being able to repeat a pattern and to continue a pattern.
- Self-care tasks, such as washing your hands, getting dressed, or brushing your teeth, are good ways to start thinking about learning sequencing skills.
- To teach your child about the sequence of things he needs to do to prepare for bedtime, chant the following:

Now it's time to wash your hands.
Now it's time to wash your hands.
What comes next?

- Ask your child what he will do next. If he says, "Brush my teeth," then chant that.
- Add the new step in the process each time.
- You can use this chant to teach your child the sequence of handwashing, of taking a bath, of getting dressed, or of any other routine.

What brain research says

During the first three years, a totally dependent child will build an incredibly complex brain that will enable him to walk, talk, analyze, care, love, play, explore, and have a unique emotional personality.

What Happens Next?

- Sit with your child, and prepare to reread one of her favorite books.
- As you reread the book, stop periodically, and ask your child what is going to happen next.
- If your child forgets or can't remember, just say something such as, "Well, let's find out."
- Keep the interaction positive and the sense of discovery alive.

What brain research says

For optimum brain development, young children need a rich and responsive language environment.

Here Comes Susie Moosey

- Say the following chant using your child's name. Find words (or make up words) that rhyme with your child's name. For example, "Here comes Bobby Dobby," "Here comes Aaron Baron," or "Here comes Jackie Wacky."

Here comes Susie Moosey
Walking down the street.
She can walk a lot of ways.
Watch her little feet.

- Suggest an action for your two-year-old to do.

Hop, Susie Moosey,
Hop, hop, hop.
You can hop down the street
With your little feet. (Hop with your child.)

- Continue, changing the actions. Additional ideas are jump, run, tiptoe, slide, skate, and march.

- This game will develop your child's listening skills and coordination.

What brain research says

Scientists are gathering more and more evidence that experiences after birth, in conjunction with what is innate, determine the eventual "wiring" of the human brain.

Author! Author!

- Encourage your child to tell you a story.
- Write the main parts of your child's story on several pieces of paper (allow space for pictures).
- Read the story back to your child.
- Let your child draw pictures to go with the text.
- Gather the pages together, and staple them into a book.
- Read your child's book to her.
- Add the book to your child's book collection.

What brain research says

Opportunities for creativity and imagination enhance the development of problem-solving skills.

Telling Stories

- Tell a familiar story with repeated phrases.
- The following dialogue from *The Three Little Pigs* is an example of phrases that are repeated in a story:

  Wolf voice: Little pig, little pig, let me come in.
  Pig voice: Not by the hair on my chinny-chin-chin.
  Wolf voice: Then I'll huff, and I'll puff, and I'll blow your house in.

- Soon your two-year-old will be able to say the words with you.
- This is fun to do with nursery rhymes. Once your child knows the words, you can begin to leave blanks and let him fill in the word. **Hint**: Begin by pausing before the last word in each line of a nursery rhyme. Because the words rhyme, they are easier to remember.
- The following are additional stories, songs, and folktales with repeated phrases.

  Brown Bear, Brown Bear, What Do You See? by Bill Martin Jr. and Eric Carle
  Caps for Sale by Esphyr Slobodkina
  The Gingerbread Man by Ronne Randall or many other authors
  Goldilocks and the Three Bears by Jan Brett or many other authors
  Miss Mary Mack by Mary Ann Hoberman or many other authors
  The Three Billy Goats Gruff by Stephen Carpenter or many other authors

What brain research says

Repetition is closely related to rhythm and rhyme, all of which are vehicles for language learning.

Favorite Poems

- Two-year-olds love the rhyme, rhythm, and emotions that words conjure up, especially in poems.
- The following are good poems to use with young children:

  "Hey Diddle Diddle"
  "Hickory Dickory Dock"
  "Humpty Dumpty"
  "Jack and Jill"
  "Jack Be Nimble"
  "Mary Had a Little Lamb"
  "Pat-a-Cake"
  "Twinkle, Twinkle, Little Star"

- Choose a poem, and say it with your two-year-old. Be dramatic, and act out the story of the nursery rhyme.
- The more dramatic and fun you make this, the more your child will enjoy it. These kinds of games will remain with your child forever.

What brain research says

A child's ability to hear and identify rhyming sounds is a basic prerequisite for reading.

Opposites Attract

- Find pictures of things that are opposites in some way, for example, hard/soft, tall/short, in/out, up/down, over/under, inside/outside, and day/night.
- Glue each picture onto cardstock to make a game of cards.
- Talk about the pictures.
- Talk about the concept of opposites, and describe how certain pictures are opposites.
- Select two or three pairs of opposite pictures.
- Mix up the cards on a table or the floor.
- Pick up a card, and ask your child to find the picture that is the opposite.
    - Reverse the game, and ask your child to pick up a card and you find the opposite.

What brain research says

Abstract concepts are best learned in playful settings.

The Music Store

- Take your two-year-old to a store that sells musical instruments.
- If you have a friendly salesperson, he or she might let your child play on the piano.
- Show your child two or three instruments. It is possible that someone in the store might be willing to demonstrate them.
- After your visit, talk with your child about the things that you saw and heard.
- When you return home, play music that uses some of the instruments that you saw at the store. Point out the sounds of the instruments you hear in the music as you listen together.

What brain research says

Hearing music stimulates a child's innate potential to learn music when she gets older.

Singing Dinner

- The more you speak to your two-year-old, the more his brain will grow.
- Singing is another way to use language. It helps your child focus on the words in a different way than when words are spoken.
- Use songs at dinnertime. Instead of asking, "Would you like some milk?" or saying, "Here is a potato," sing or chant the sentence.
- This is marvelous fun.

What brain research says

Neural plasticity, the brain's ability to adapt with experience, supports the idea that early stimulation impacts how children will continue to learn and interact with others throughout life.

Sing Along

- Watch for a concert in your area by a children's music artist.
- Before attending the event, talk with your child about what will happen—music, movement, and participation.
- Let your child know that she is welcome to clap, sing, and move as part of the concert.
- While at the concert, participate in the musical experience along with your child.
- When the concert is over, talk about the songs your child liked.

What brain research says

Early stimulation sets the stage for how children will continue to learn and interact with others throughout life.

Sorting Toys

- Two-year-olds love their toys. The more you can play games that involve their toys, the more they will enjoy it.
- Sit on the floor with your two-year-old, and put some toys in front of you.
- Start sorting the toys by color. "Let's find all of the toys that have the color red and put them together." Continue sorting by color.
- You can sort by size, color, or characteristics (toys that have wheels, animal toys, and so on).
- Ask your child how he thinks the toys should be sorted. You and your child will figure out many ways by looking at the toys.
- This game develops your child's thinking skills.

What brain research says

Children love to play. It comes naturally to them and is something they should be encouraged to do because it is essential to their development. Gross motor skills, fine motor skills, thinking skills—everything is learned through play.

Playing Hopscotch

- Draw a simple hopscotch grid on the sidewalk, and number it up to five.
- Show your two-year-old how to throw a marker on one of the numbers. Use a pebble, a stick, or anything that is not too small and not sharp.
- Ask your child to hop to that number.
- You can also ask her to jump, run, or march to the designated number.
- This game develops your child's coordination, balance, and counting skills.

What brain research says

Movement integrates the right and left hemispheres of young learners' brains.

Name the Color

- Tie several scarves together, and put them in an empty tissue box.
- Let your child pull the scarves out of the box. He will love doing this!
- Put the scarves in the box again.
- This time ask your child to find a scarf with the color red.
- As he pulls out the scarves, he may find more than one scarf with the color red.
- This is a great game to play to help children learn about colors.
- Repeat with other colors.
- You can also play this game by putting scarves in an empty paper towel roll.

What brain research says

The excitement of discovery will stimulate your little one's curiosity.

Doing Chores

- Two-year-olds love to be given responsibilities.
- Talk with your little one about things that she can do to help. For example, take the dishes out of the dishwasher, put away the cereal in the pantry, or get herself dressed.
- Look through magazines together, and find pictures of chores that your child can do.
- Cut out the pictures, and paste them on small cards that your little one can hold in her hand.
- Put the cards in a box, and let her select a card and do the chore.
- This game builds your child's self-esteem.

What brain research says

Offering varied activities for play and exploring with real objects, people, and things in nature allows the brain to figure out how things in the world work.

Giants and Fairies

- Show your two-year-old how to take giant steps.
- Now show him how to take little, tiny fairy steps.
- Make up a story using these two characters, and each time you mention one of them, you and your child take either a giant step or a fairy step.
- Here is an idea to begin a story:

Once upon a time there was a big giant who lived on a hill. He had many playmates, but his favorite was the teeny, tiny fairy…

- Make up the rest of the story.

What brain research says

Creativity and imagination are higher-level skills. It is critical to provide opportunities for all young children to develop these valuable skills.

Laundry Baskets

- Laundry baskets are great targets for practicing throwing skills.
- Experiment with different objects like balls, wadded paper, and scarves to throw into the basket.
- Each object will require a different kind of motor skill to get it into the basket.
- Place the basket close enough to your child so that she will be successful in getting the object into the basket.
- This is a great way to develop coordination.

What brain research says

When learning new skills, each move has to be repeated over and over to strengthen neural circuits.

Colored Ice

- Make ice cubes using water mixed with food coloring.
- Start with one color.
- Put the ice cubes in a dishpan or an unbreakable bin.
- Engage in play with the ice cubes. Use the color of the ice cubes in conversation: "Please give me a blue ice cube."
- Use the ice cubes as blocks, and try stacking them. Watching them melt is lots of fun. The melting will be a trigger for questions from your child and for more conversation.
- Make a second batch of ice cubes using two colors. Name the colors of the ice cubes, and describe the colors as you stack them.
- When these ice cubes melt, you may have a different color. For example, if you are using red and yellow ice cubes, you may have orange liquid when they melt.
- Perfect for a hot day!

What brain research says

The brain is a self-organizing organ. Existing connections eagerly await new experiences that shape the neural networks for language, reasoning, problem solving, and moral values.

More Colored Ice

- Make ice cubes with water and food coloring in the primary colors of blue, yellow, and red.
- Once the ice cubes are formed, place two of the colored ice cubes (each a different color) in a ziplock bag.
- Ask your child to move the ice around and watch as it melts.
- As the two colors melt, a new color will be formed.
- Tell your child the name of the new color that is formed as the cubes melt together.
- Extend this activity by giving your child fingerpaint in two different primary colors.
- Place a dollop of each color on some fingerpaint paper.
- Suggest that your child mix the colors together and see what happens.
- Remind your child of what happened with the melted colored ice and now with the paint.

What brain research says

New experiences build upon established patterns and create new patterns and networks for more learning.

Colorful Steps

- Tape a construction-paper path on a floor.
- Use two or three different colors in your path.
- Sing one of your child's favorite songs as you and your two-year-old walk on the path. "Twinkle, Twinkle, Little Star" is a good song to use.
- From time to time, stop singing, and then stop walking. If your child knows colors, ask him to name the color of the construction paper that you are standing on.
- Develop your child's spatial thinking by suggesting, "Let's walk over the paper," "Let's walk on the paper," or "Let's walk around the paper."
- You can also do other actions such as hopping, jumping, and tiptoeing along the path.

What brain research says

During critical brain-growth periods, long, thin fibers grow inside the brain, creating pathways that carry electrical impulses from cell to cell. The resulting network, which grows daily in the young brain, forms the neurological foundation upon which a child builds a lifetime of skills.

Chalk Line

- Provide your child with a large piece of black construction paper.
- Give your child several pieces of colored chalk.
- Let her explore using the chalk on the construction paper.
- Help your child notice how vibrant the colors look.
- If you have a sidewalk or know of a place where sidewalk-chalk drawing is permitted, encourage your child to use the sidewalk as a canvas and to draw with the chalk on the sidewalk. (Remind your child that this is done only with permission.)

What brain research says

Extending patterns of learning by using new materials and experiences promotes problem-solving and reasoning skills.

A Rhythm Game

- Say the following chant, and do the actions:

  One, two, three,
  Touch your knee.
  One, two, three,
  Knee, knee, knee.

- Repeat, changing the part of the body. For example, touch your arm or touch your toe.
- The words do not have to rhyme.
- Children learn an awareness of rhythm.

What brain research says

Exposure to music, rhythm, and rhyme rewires neural circuits and strengthens those used in mathematics.

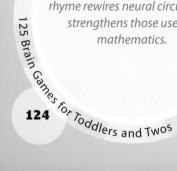

Where Is Jack?

● Say the following rhyme and do the actions, then ask your two-year-old to join you:

I'm a little box (Stoop down with your arms hugging your head.)
Still as can be. (Stay very still.)
Lift up my lid, (Slowly raise your hands above your head.)
And what do you see?
Shhh! Boo! (Jump up, and raise your hands high in the air.)
Jack in the box!

What brain research says

Each young brain forms the neuronal and muscular connections required for sitting and crawling, walking and talking at its own pace.

What's That Print?

- Gather together a variety of objects that can make distinctive prints—spools, craft feathers, sponges, small toys, pinecones, small leaves, and any other object in your environment.
- Give your child a large piece of paper.
- On a separate paper plate, place dollops of different colors of tempera paint.
- Show your child the objects.
- Help your child dip the objects into the paint and make simple prints on the paper.
- Allow the prints to dry.
- Talk about the prints, and compare them with the objects your child used to make them.
- Use a marker or pen, and write the name of the object under or beside the print it made.

What brain research says

Abstract thinking is enhanced by language—it is the process by which experience becomes knowledge.

Muffin Man Rhymes

- Sing the following to the tune of "Do You Know the Muffin Man?"

  Do you know the jo, jo, jo
  Ho, ho, ho
  Go, go, go
  Do you know the jo, jo, jo
  Ho, ho, go, go, go, hey!

- As you sing the song, dance around, and clap your hands on the word *hey.*
- Pick any three rhyming sounds to sing the song.
- This helps your little one learn about rhyming.

What brain research says

Scans of children's brains show that the growth at this age is explosive, a fact that allows them to absorb and organize new information at a rate much faster than adults' brains.

It's Just Puzzling

- Select a drawing or painting that your child has done.
- Ask your child if it would be okay to turn the drawing or painting into a puzzle. (Do not assume your child will not care if his picture is cut up. If he objects, use picture from a magazine or catalog.)

- When you have determined that it is okay to make the drawing or painting into a puzzle, glue the picture onto a piece of cardstock or poster board.
- Once the glue has dried, turn the picture over, and draw some simple puzzle-shape lines on the back. Making it into four or five simple puzzle shapes will be best.
- Cut out the puzzle by following the lines.
- Turn the pieces over, and mix them up.
- Encourage your child to put the puzzle of his picture back together.

What brain research says

Puzzles involve reasoning, discrimination, and muscle control, which all challenge the developing brain.

What Was That?

- Select two or three fruits or vegetables to sample for a snack.
- Cut up the fruits and vegetables into small, bite-sized pieces for your child.
- Place the pieces on a plate.
- Review the items with your child so she is familiar with what is on the plate.
- Tell your child to close her eyes and to pick a piece with her eyes closed.
- Ask your child to identify what she is eating.

What brain research says

Learning to pay attention is a skill that is essential to almost all other learning.

Musical Instruments

- Provide an assortment of rhythm instruments for your two-year-old to explore.
- Start with a drum, sand blocks, a triangle, and sticks.

  - Drum: Hit it on the rim, then hit it in the middle. One sound will be higher, and the other one lower.
  - Sand blocks: Rub them together to hear an interesting sound like a train.
  - Triangle: Hit it at different places to produce higher and lower sounds.
    - Sticks: Hit them on different surfaces to produce different sounds. Hitting a stick on the floor and then on a table will be fascinating to your child.

What brain research says

Exposure to music rewires neural circuits. Like other circuits formed early in life, the ones for music will endure.

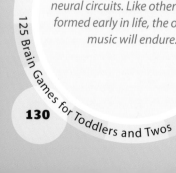

130

125 Brain Games for Toddlers and Twos

Grocery Shopping

- Ask your child to help you prepare a grocery list.
- Take him to the supermarket, and look for the items on the list.
- When you return home, let your child help you put away the groceries by reading to him the labels, box tops, and packages as you store them.
- Make a recipe with the ingredients that you bought at the store.
- Tell your child that you appreciate his help. Say something such as, "You really helped a lot today with all the grocery shopping and putting things away. I like going shopping with you."

What brain research says

In the course of the first three years, a totally dependent infant will build an incredibly complex brain that will be the beginning of an independent child.

Sing, Jump, and Stop

- Tell your two-year-old that you are going to sing a song and jump at the same time. Whenever you stop singing, it is also time to stop jumping.
- Sing a familiar song like "Row, Row, Row Your Boat," and jump. Stop at any time during the song.
- It is best to sing just one or two lines at the beginning so that your child will understand how the game works.
- Let your child choose the song and the activity—jump, march, hop, run, and so on.
- This game is great fun.

What brain research says

Physical play stimulates the part of the brain that regulates emotions. This leads to better management of stress and emotions.

Cross-Lateral Fun

- Sing the following to the tune of the "Pawpaw Patch":

Where, oh, where is hungry little (child's name)?
Where, oh, where is hungry little (child's name)?
Where, oh, where is hungry little (child's name)?
Way down yonder in the veggie patch.

- Pretend you are walking in a garden full of vegetables. Each time you name one of them, you pretend to pick it up and put it in a pretend basket.
- The trick is that you always use the opposite arm to pick the vegetable. If the vegetable is on the right side, you use the left hand to pick it up. If it is on the left side, you use the right hand to pick it up.
- Sing the following:

Pick up spinach, and put it in the basket.
Pick up spinach, and put it in the basket.
Pick up spinach, and put it in the basket.
Way down yonder in the veggie patch.

- Continue on with tomatoes, beans, cauliflower, broccoli, and other vegetables that are familiar to your child.

What brain research says

It is important to build cross-lateral exercises into your day. Cross-lateral movements are movements where the arms and legs cross over from one side of the body to the other. The left side of the brain controls the right side of the body, and the right side of the brain controls the left side. Both sides are forced to communicate when arms and legs cross over. Cross-lateral movements "unstick" the brain and energize learning.

Brain Break Exercise

- This activity will get the blood flowing and will release tension and stress.
- Say the poem "The Grand Old Duke of York," and do the actions.
- Start slowly, and try to increase the speed. Lots of fun!

The grand old Duke of York, (March in place.)
He had ten thousand men. (Keep marching.)
He marched them up the hill, (March in place with hands high above your head.)
And then he marched them down again. (March with bended knees.)
And when you're up, you're up, (March with hands high in the air.)
And when you're down, you're down, (March with bended knees.)
And when you're only halfway up, (March halfway up.)
You're neither up (Hold hands high.)
Nor down. (March with bended knees.)

What brain research says

According to Eric Jensen, the author of Brain-Based Learning, *children need to stand up and stretch to "exercise" their brains.*

Rainstick Game

- Show your two-year-old a rainstick.
- Tip it back and forth to let her see how it works and hear how it sounds.
- As you move it, sing a rain song.

  Rain, rain, go away,
  Come again another day.
  Little (child's name) *wants to play.*
  Rain, please go away.

- Give the rainstick to your little one, and let her tip it back and forth as you sing the song.
- Sing other rain songs such as "It's Raining, It's Pouring" and "The Itsy, Bitsy Spider."

What brain research says

Quality musical experiences enhance listening skills and help children learn about rhythm and beat. This helps children learn vocabulary and memory skills.

References and Resources

Books

Bergen, D. and J. Coscia. 2001. *Brain research and early childhood education: Implications for educators.* Olney, MD: Association for Childhood Education International.

Brown, S. 2009. *Play: How it shapes the brain, opens the imagination, and invigorates the soul.* New York: Penguin.

Caine, G. and R. Caine. 2009. *Making connections: Teaching and the human brain.* Chicago: Addison-Wesley.

Carnegie Corporation of New York. 1994. *Starting points: Meeting the needs of our youngest children.* New York: Carnegie Corporation.

Eliot, L. 2000. *What's going on in there? How the brain and mind develop in the first five years of life.* New York: Bantam.

Eliot, L. 2010. *Pink brain, blue brain: How small differences grow into troublesome gaps—And what we can do about it.* New York: Mariner Books.

Elkind, D. 2000. *The power of play: How spontaneous, imaginative activities lead to happier, healthier children.* Cambridge, MA: Da Capo Press.

Gardner, H. 1983. *Frames of mind: The theory of multiple intelligences.* New York: Basic Books.

Gerhardt, S. 2004. *Why love matters: How affection shapes a baby's brain.* New York: Routledge.

Goodwin, S. and L. Acredolo. 2005. *Baby hearts: A guide to giving your child an emotional head start.* New York: Bantam.

Gopnik, A., A. N. Meltzoff, and P. K. Kuhl. 2000. *The scientist in the crib: What early learning tells us about the mind.* New York: HarperCollins.

Gordon, M. 2005. *The roots of empathy: Changing the world child by child*. Toronto: Thomas Allen Publishers.

Hirsh-Pasek, K. and R. M. Golinkoff. 2005. *Einstein never used flashcards*. Emmaus, PA: Rodale.

Howard, P. J. 1994. *The owners' manual for the brain: Everyday application from mind-brain research*. Austin, TX: Leornian Press.

Kotulak, R. 1996. *Inside the brain: Revolutionary discoveries of how the mind works*. Kansas City, MO: Andrews and McNeel.

Langer, E. J. 1997. *The power of mindful learning*. Cambridge, MA: Da Capo Press.

Medina, J. 2010. *Brain rules for baby: How to raise a smart and happy child from zero to five*. Seattle, WA: Pear Press.

Medina, J. 2011. *Brain rules: 12 principles for surviving and thriving at work, home, and school.* Seattle, WA: Pear Press.

Riley, D., R. R. San Juan, J. Klinkner, and A. Ramminger. 2008. *Social & emotional development: Connecting science and practice in early childhood settings*. St. Paul, MN: Redleaf Press.

Schiller, P. 1999. *Start smart: Building brain power in the early years*. Beltsville, MD: Gryphon House.

Shore, R. 1997. *Rethinking the brain: New insights into early development*. New York: Families and Work Institute.

Silberg, J. 2002. *Games to play with babies,* third edition. Beltsville, MD: Gryphon House.

Silberg, J. 2002. *Games to play with toddlers*, revised. Beltsville, MD: Gryphon House.

Silberg, J. 2002. *Games to play with two year olds,* revised. Beltsville, MD: Gryphon House.

Silberg, J. 2009. *Baby smarts: Games for playing and learning.* Beltsville, MD: Gryphon House.

Sylwester, R. 1995. *A Celebration of neurons: An educator's guide

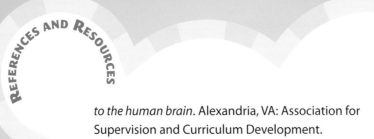

to the human brain. Alexandria, VA: Association for Supervision and Curriculum Development.

Websites

Better Brains for Babies. http://www.fcs.uga.edu/ext/bbb
BrainNet. http://www.brainnet.org
The Dana Foundation. http://www.dana.org/
Talaris Research Institute. http://www.talaris.org
Zero to Three: National Center for Infants, Toddlers, and Families. http://www.zerotothree.org

DVDs and Videos

Can you pass the all-time great parent test? Chicago: McCormick Tribune Foundation. 49 min.

Blakemore, B. and P. Jennings. "Common miracles: The new American revolution in learning." *ABC News Special*. Directed by Peter George, aired January 23, 1993. DVD/VHS, 60 min.

Brazelton, T. B. *10 things every child needs for the best start in life*.

Kuhl, P. *The linguistic genius of babies*. Filmed October 2010. TED video, 10:18. Posted February 2011. http://www.ted.com/talks/patricia_kuhl_the_linguistic_genius_of_babies.html

Perry, B. "Dr. Bruce Perry, childhood development on LIVING SMART with Patricia Gras." YouTube video, 26:41, from *Houston PBS Living Smart*, posted by "HoustonPBS," March 15, 2010, http://www.youtube.com/watch?v=vak-iDwZJY8

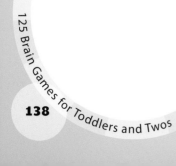

Reiner, R. *The first years last forever.* From the I Am Your Child
video series. Produced by Parents' Action for Children
and Rob Reiner. May 1, 2005. DVD, 30 min.

Articles

Begley, S.1997. How to build a baby's brain. *Newsweek,*
Spring/Summer, special ed.

Brownlee, S.1998. Baby talk. *U.S. News and World Report,*
June 15.

Caine, R. N., G. Caine, C. L. McClintic, and K. J. Klimek. 2004.
12 Brain/Mind learning principles in action—One
author's personal journey. *New Horizons for Learning.*

Graziano, A., M. Peterson, and G. Shaw. 1999. Enhanced
learning of proportional math through music training
and spatial-temporal training. *Neurological Research*:
139–152.

Highfield, R. 2008. Harvard's baby brain research lab. *The
Telegraph,* April 30.

Nash, M. 1997. Fertile minds. *Time,* February 3.

Newberger, J. J. 1997. New brain development research: A
wonderful opportunity to build public support for early
childhood education. *Young Children,* 4–9.

Swidley, N. 2007. Rush, little baby. *Boston Globe,* October 28.

Zigler, E. *Pre to 3: Policy implications of child brain
development.* Testimony given to U.S. Senate Labor and
Human Resources Committee, Subcommittee on
Children and Families. Washington, DC, June 5, 1997.

Index

125 Brain Games for Toddlers and Twos